Edit

A Forgotten Heroine

Nick Miller

Keeper of the Cavell Memorabilia
for St Mary's Church, Swardeston, Norfolk

GROVE BOOKS LIMITED
RIDLEY HALL RD CAMBRIDGE CB3 9HU

Contents

Acknowledgments

I owe especial thanks to: Jan, my late wife; Ginny, my second wife, and my daughters Lydia and Emily, all of whom have walked with me on the Cavell journey; Kim and Penelope Swithinbank and their Retreat Centre at The Vine, Hullavington, Wiltshire; the Rt Rev'd Robert Innes of Holy Trinity Church Brussels, and now Bishop of Gibraltar in Europe; the Rev'd Philip Seddon, former Chair of the Grove Spirituality Group; Natalie Strange; and many who have listened to the telling of the story and asked helpful questions.

The website www.edithcavell.org.uk has fuller background material, including the full text of hymns Edith Cavell would have drawn on, further biblical material and other reflections. Reactions to this booklet or the web material can be emailed to enquiry@edithcavell.org.uk.

First Impression November 2014
ISSN 0262–799X
ISBN 978 1 85174 919 5

Introduction: Starting at the End...

There was no need for her to be woken in her prison cell at 5 o'clock that morning; she was already dressed. Prison guards stood in silence as she was escorted through the corridors. At the firing range two newly painted white posts confronted the English woman, 49 years old, 5'3" and greying, as well as her co-worker, a younger Belgian man. Two squads of eight soldiers stood about two metres away. The Belgian man addressed the soldiers, 'Good day, gentlemen. In the face of death we are all comrades. Long live Belgium.' The woman said to her chaplain, 'My conscience is clear. I die for God and for my country.' The order sounded: 'Fire!' Both were quickly confirmed as dead, and were buried where they had fallen. The German chaplain commented later, 'She went to her death with a bearing which is quite impossible to forget.'

When was this? Who were the pair executed? What brought them to this end?

The executions were carried out by German soldiers near Brussels at 7am on Tuesday, 12 October, 1915. The woman executed was Edith Cavell, a nurse from Norfolk, who had been running a training school for nurses in Brussels before and during the German occupation of Belgium in 1914. She was shot for her part in helping at least 200 allied soldiers escape to neutral Holland. The Belgian man was Philippe Baucq, a key part of the network, helping soldiers out to Holland and publishing an underground newspaper.

Edith Cavell's story has largely been forgotten. There are several biographies; but none deal fully with her faith.[1] This booklet tells the story, alongside material from the Bible and Thomas à Kempis' *Of the Imitation of Christ*. These would have been very familiar, 'carried' in her head and on her heart. She annotated à Kempis through her weeks in prison.[2] I have recently read this for the first time: I now understand better what shaped her way of living. Each chapter starts with a statement by her and a parallel à Kempis quotation.

I have 'walked with' Edith for twenty years here in 'her' village of Swardeston. The more I have thought about her, the more her lived faith has shaped my own. Her courage and her commitment to what she believed to be her Christian duty challenge and inspire me. She would no doubt have pointed to her own shortcomings. These I have tried to report even-handedly; they make her life all the more inspiring. I tell her story and suggest reflections on her, hoping that others will be challenged to follow her in 'imitating Christ.'

2

'I Am Going To Do Something Useful—Something For People'[3]

May I be made fit to love, courageous to suffer, steady to persevere.[4]

Edith Cavell once wrote to her cousin Eddy Cavell, 'Some day I am going to do something useful—something for people. They are most of them so helpless, so hurt and so unhappy.'[5]

Florence Nightingale, 45 years her senior, would have echoed the same sentiment. Both were women of character and drive, wanting to play a significant part in making theirs a better world. The quotation is no doubt common as a youthful aspiration, but the added significance in the lives of Nightingale and Cavell is that they broke the mould of Victorian middle-class expectations for unmarried women and blazed a trail for future generations.

Edith Cavell grew up in a Norfolk country vicarage until she was sixteen, educated by her father alongside her three younger siblings. Hers was an idyllic childhood and her talents were given free rein—she was an accomplished artist, played the piano and sang, played tennis, skated on a neighbour's pond and taught Sunday school.

The relative privilege of her background was tempered by her awareness of the real world in the village and wider community; she and her sisters would take Sunday dinner to impoverished homes before the family sat down to eat. Her father was chaplain to the workhouse in Swainsthorpe, an adjacent village, which served the wider area. Edith Cavell would have been well aware of the difficulties of the poor who were hovering on the borderline of being sent to the workhouse and of those who did spend time there—orphans, single parents, people with mental health problems, those with learning and physical disabilities, the old and infirm. She was alert to how many were 'so helpless.'

She trained as a teaching assistant and became a governess, as so many of her background would have done, having little parental income on which to rely. She looked after many children in well-off homes in England before spending five years as governess to a French family in Brussels. Meanwhile, both her younger sisters chose to train as nurses, and were 'doing something useful.'[6]

Having spent time in 1895 looking after her father who was bed-bound in Swardeston she chose, aged thirty, to begin a new chapter in her life, doing something more 'useful for people' by enrolling as a probationer nurse.

There are descriptions of her as an adult—she was 5′ 3″, slightly built and slender, with swept-back dark hair (which later turned grey), dark eyebrows, nose slightly tilted and high-chiselled cheekbones. She was described by one of the boys under her care as a 'martinet,' but was much loved.[7] She was always well turned out, but at her first meeting with a new colleague she was perceived as 'rather withdrawn, uninterested in superficial friendships, but thoughtful, pleasant and sympathetic to all her patients.'[8]

Edith Cavell chose to train in London, and in what was probably its toughest area. She enrolled in 1896 at the London Hospital in Whitechapel in the East End. The matron, Miss Eva Luckes, ran the nursing establishment of over 600 nurses. She was not overly impressed with Edith Cavell: 'She had plenty of capability for her work…but she was not very much in earnest, not at all punctual and not a nurse that could be altogether depended on. She had a self-sufficient manner.'[9]

A London Hospital contemporary recalled, 'We were awakened by the ringing of a bell at 6am. Breakfast at 6.30am, on duty at 7am (after prayers), with half an hour for dinner, tea on the ward, two hours off duty during the day and supper when we came off duty at 9.20pm, and so to bed—tired and weary—lights out at 10pm. As probationers we had a day off once a fortnight and two weeks' holiday a year.[10] We had to attend lectures in our precious off-duty time.'[11]

After four years at the London Hospital she moved on, eventually to more senior posts mainly in Poor Law establishments in the East End and finally in Manchester, where she led a team engaged in community nursing. All her postings were in very needy areas, among people living in impoverished communities and with a range of associated health conditions like tuberculosis, bronchitis, smallpox and under-nourishment.

She took her nursing very seriously. Medicine was emerging as a new science with the advent of penicillin and X-rays. She wanted the partner profession of nursing to develop along the same scientific lines, based on knowledge, not just on past practice. She wanted to be making a difference in training and supervising new entrants to her profession, serving the community and working as a team with doctors and almoners (hospital social workers).

Personal Reflection

Edith Cavell's Vision

'Doing something useful for people' is one possible life goal. How do we choose between life goals, for example, 'to make a million before I'm 40,' 'win gold in a sport,' 'change the world' and so on?

- What have my life's goals been so far? What—or who—am I living for now? Is this rewarding?

Her Formation
Edith Cavell had powerful Christian role models; she was shaped by the Bible, the *Book of Common Prayer*, poetry, *Of the Imitation of Christ*, and hymns.

- What has shaped and formed my life—negatively and positively?

Her Choices
She made a key choice when starting nursing training for four years as a mature adult aged 30. She had to leave home, follow her call and follow God's call on her life.

Later she worked within the ethos of the Victorian Poor Law. This could be punitive (with the emphasis on deterring fecklessness and keeping the local tax rates down). She will have had to work out how to reconcile this with the love and care she would have as a set of core values, both as a nurse and a Christian.

- What parallel choice(s) have I made? What other choices have I made? Have they worked out well?

Linked Material
Jesus invited the first disciples, 'Come, follow me' (Matt 4.18–22). They, like Edith, had little idea where their 'following' might lead.

> Supplement your faith with a generous provision of moral excellence, and moral excellence with knowledge, and knowledge with self-control, and self-control with patient endurance, and patient endurance with godliness, and godliness with brotherly affection, and brotherly affection with love for everyone. The more you grow like this, the more productive and useful you will be in your knowledge of our Lord Jesus Christ. (2 Pet 1.5–8, Living Bible)

'My Duty Is With My Nurses' (in Brussels)[12]

3

Labour but now a little, and thou shalt find great rest, yea, perpetual joy.[13]

In summer 1914 Edith Cavell was in charge of a training school for nurses in Brussels. Here she had pioneered the training of professional nurses in Belgium for nearly seven years. Hitherto nursing had been done by untrained nuns. She had been invited to take up this post by a progressive surgeon, Dr Depage, who had set up a *clinique* with beds, training facilities and nurses' accommodation close to the hospital where he was working. A group of four nurses started their training with Edith Cavell in October 1907; by 1913 there were over three hundred trained nurses across Brussels.

Each summer Edith Cavell always made sure she could get home to her mother in Norfolk for a holiday.[14] She was in Norfolk for the second half of July 1914. War was looming and on 1 August a telegram reached her concerning imminent German invasion. She was urged to get back or she might not be able to return. What was she to do?

Should she stay in England? Her mother was aged 78 (she had been widowed in 1910) and needed care.[15] There would be many nursing opportunities at home as soldiers were invalided back to England. Some said any war might be over by Christmas. She knew there would be significant risks to herself if she returned to Belgium.

Should she head back to Brussels? There was a clear need for nursing leadership in Brussels. She was under contract and had many responsibilities, managing her *clinique*, training nurses and doctors, overseeing the building of a new training establishment and advising other nursing services. She was responsible for two vulnerable young women whom she had invited to live with her: Grace Jemmett, a young friend of her family who had become addicted to morphine after an operation and had been living with Edith Cavell for five years, and Pauline Randall, a sixteen year old girl who was 'adopted' by Edith Cavell when she had been abandoned by her father who worked in a circus.

She decided to return to Brussels: 'My duty is with my nurses.' She boarded a train in Norwich and took the night ferry from Harwich to Ostend on 2

August 1914. The Germans marched into Belgium on 3 August and, having issued an ultimatum which Germany ignored, Great Britain was formally at war at 11pm London time on 4 August. Meanwhile, 200,000 Belgians flooded across the Channel to seek asylum in England.

Personal Reflection

What Is In It for Me?
As with so many Victorians, Edith Cavell had a strong sense of duty. As a nurse she will have understood the profession as a vocation. As a Christian disciple she will have felt that God had led her into nursing and into her place in Brussels and, unless he specifically called her elsewhere, she would remain obedient to that calling. Her faith and nursing vocation were inseparable.

- To whom am I subject? To whom do I owe allegiance? How free am I to change my allegiances?

Finding a Way of Life
There are many potential sources of wisdom, perhaps more easily available today than ever before. Edith Cavell sought to follow Jesus, drawing on the advice of Thomas à Kempis, and her colleagues. Sometimes these will have conflicted; sometimes the Christian way seemed unwisely self-denying or unworldly.

- What is the source of my wisdom? How do I look to God for that?

Linked Material

God gave Moses and Joshua the promise of his continuing presence: 'My presence will go with you' (Exod 33.14); 'The Lord your God will go with you wherever you go' (Joshua 1.9).

Returning to Brussels, Edith Cavell may have recalled Jesus' own determination to go to Jerusalem, knowing that he was likely to be arrested and killed ('He steadfastly set his face to go to Jerusalem' (Luke 9.51, AV)), and his warning that, 'No one who puts his hand to the plough and looks back is fit for the kingdom of God' (Luke 9.62).

'We Were Divided Between Pity and Hatred' (for the German troops)[16]

Keep silence in an evil time and inwardly turn thyself to me: be not troubled by the judgment of men.[17]

Background

In August 1914 the German advance towards Paris had been terrible. Belgian neutrality had been totally ignored. Belgian men signed up for the army, leaving their loved ones behind. Many others headed into France or neutral Holland or across the Channel to Britain. Dr Depage set up a major hospital on the coast to receive the wounded. He asked Edith to come with him, but she decided to stay in Brussels to oversee the continuing work there and to prepare for the wounded. Eighteen thousand beds in makeshift hospitals linked to the Red Cross were prepared from voluntary donations and volunteers were hastily trained as nursing assistants.

The noise of gunfire in the east could be heard in the streets, and flames were often visible at night. Nurses would gather in Edith Cavell's sitting room for their customary evening talks with their matron. How did she see their role? 'Any wounded soldier must be treated, friend or foe. Each man is a father, husband or son. As nurses you must take no part in the quarrel—our work is for humanity. The profession of nursing knows no frontiers.'[18]

The German troops marched in to Brussels on 20 August. Edith wrote in her despatch to the *Nursing Mirror*, 'We were divided between *pity* for these poor fellows, far from their country and their people, suffering the weariness and fatigue of an arduous campaign, and *hate* of a vindictive foe bringing ruin and desolation on hundreds of happy homes and to a prosperous and peaceful land.'[19]

Personal Reflection

As Christians, we are commanded to love our enemies and to do good to those who persecute us (Luke 6.27–28). Watching the weary and disoriented German army arriving, Edith Cavell saw every man as 'someone's son, husband or father.' This generous, inclusive response to other human beings took her far beyond what might, for many Belgians, have been automatic repugnance and hatred. But unease, outrage, even anger and hatred were still instinctive reactions towards the occupation.

She needed to remain honest in confronting this instinctive response in the light of Jesus' demands to love the invaders.

- In what situations do my instinctive responses clash with the demands of my faith/my values?

Linked Material

Jesus had compassion for the crowds (Matt 9.26) and taught that we must love our enemy (Matt 5.44). The Parable of the Good Samaritan is a key and radical parable about *being*, in the new kingdom of God, a merciful neighbour to someone who may turn out to be our enemy (Luke 10.30–37).

5

'Show the Two Men In'[20]

> It is God's will that we become fully obedient to him and that we overcome mere reason on the wings of a burning love for him.[21]

In late August and September 1914 the German army advanced rapidly towards Paris. This left many French and British soldiers stranded behind the advancing German line. Notices in French were posted everywhere by the occupying German army: 'Hand over any allied soldier to the authorities or be shot.' Soldiers in civilian clothes could be shot as spies.

Edith Cavell continued her nursing work in Brussels, but was well aware of the dangers. There were many Germans in plain clothes looking for spies and seeking out those who infringed the draconian laws imposed by the occupiers. Some Belgians were known to be informers, too.

On 1 November 1914 two wounded British soldiers in civilian clothes, accompanied by a Belgian mining engineer, came to the *clinique*. They had been sent to Edith Cavell by her friend and colleague, Mme Marie Depage, who was in charge of the nurses at the Royal Palace hospital. She had no way of caring for them but sent them to the *clinique* as a last hope. They were Colonel Boger and Sergeant Meachin of the Cheshire Regiment. They had been in hiding on the Belgian/French border since being cut off from their colleagues in late August after the Battle of Mons. They had been captured in a field hospital which was taken over by the Germans. When it was clear they were destined for a prisoner of war camp in Germany they had escaped together. Both had been looked after by local people despite the great risk to themselves.

There is no recorded evidence of hesitation on Edith Cavell's part: 'Show the two men in.' She hid them in the basement of the *clinique* and arranged for Colonel Boger to be operated on. She then planned help to get them away to neutral Holland with the necessary papers and funds.[22]

Personal Reflection

War always involves disorientation for combatants, for families, for those occupied. For the latter the likelihood of receiving justice from occupiers is limited.

- How might I have reacted to being under occupation?

Edith Cavell must have thought in advance about how she should react to allied soldiers seeking her help. It was clearly illegal—it carried the death penalty. It was also risky to her whole *clinique* operation and to her colleagues. But she knew that if she refused to harbour such men they might be caught in Brussels and could be shot. She knew others had already risked their lives getting men from southern Belgium to the centre of the city. Once she talked to the two men she would have been even more aware that there would be more fugitive soldiers following in their path. Was she prepared to hand them all over and then to learn that any or all had been executed? She decided to take the two soldiers in (and by extension to be part of the continuing covert operation), and she nursed them herself.

- Have I faced a costly and morally ambiguous choice? In Edith Cavell's circumstances would I have put my life on the line?

Linked Material

Edith Cavell disobeyed the law. Edmund Burke (1727–1797) comments, 'It is not what a lawyer tells me I may do, but what humanity, reason and justice tell me I ought to do…'

Thomas à Kempis writes, 'Man considereth the deeds, but God weigheth the intentions.'[23]

Whoever sees his brother in need and has no pity on him, how can the love of God dwell in him? (1 John 3.15)

Jesus is pictured in Revelation: 'Here I am! I stand at the door and knock. If anyone hears my voice and opens the door I will come in and eat with him and he with me' (Rev 3.20). If Edith had heard Jesus knocking and asked him into her own life, could she then bar the door to others in need whom the same Jesus loved and died for?

When the Jewish religious authorities ruled that the early Christians were not to speak of Jesus, Peter as a Jew should have obeyed them—but he replied, 'We must obey God rather than any human authority' (Acts 5.29, NRSV).

'Don't Send Any More Men—If One Were Shot it Would Be Our Fault'[24]

6

> Put all thy trust in God…He shall answer for thee and will do in all things what is best for thee.[25]

By May 1915 Edith Cavell had helped a large number of men in the basement of her *clinique*.[26] More were still coming to Brussels, helped by brave French and Belgian civilians in defiance of the occupiers. Edith Cavell regularly smuggled individuals or small groups through the streets in the early morning or late evening. She helped arrange the necessary papers and disguises for the men.

All this was putting her life at risk: German soldiers were everywhere. Each time she went out she and the men could be stopped and questioned. People associated with the *clinique* could give the operation away at any time. She was under huge pressure. Her deputy, now aware of the men being hidden, was trying to get her to stop but to no avail. Edith could not, in good conscience, live with the consequences 'if one were caught and shot'; she must play whatever part she could to save all who came to her for help.

She was arrested in early August, along with nearly forty suspects from the underground network. She was transferred to Brussels' St Gilles prison on 7 August and placed in solitary confinement. She confessed openly under interrogation; perhaps she was tricked (her interrogators assured her others had told the whole story), or perhaps it was her instinctively truthful nature?

Personal Reflection

Was Edith Cavell stupid to have persisted in hiding and spiriting the allied soldiers out of Brussels? Should the soldiers not have surrendered? She could have gone home. Was she naïve in her confession, implicating others? She had to weigh up the risk to her against that of others. Did she feel this was part of her vocation as a nurse and her calling as an obedient follower of Christ?

> • If I were faced with similar moral challenges would I both think and act that radically?

Linked Material

'We can rejoice when we run into problems and trials—they help us learn to be patient. And patience develops strength of character in us and helps us trust God more each time we use it until finally our hope and faith are strong and steady. Then we are able to hold our heads high no matter what happens and know that all is well, for we know how dearly God loves us' (Rom 5.3–5, *Living Bible*).

7

'I Thank God for These Ten Weeks of Quiet'[27]

> Those carried by God's grace travel easily…do not feel weary and are led by the greatest of leaders.[28]

On the night before she was to be shot, Edith Cavell spoke of the benefit of her 'weeks of quiet' to the Rev'd Stirling Gahan, the chaplain at her church in Brussels, in her prison cell.[29]

She had been alone in Cell 23 in St Gilles prison for nearly ten weeks. The only time she had been allowed out was for exercise in the prison yard for thirty minutes daily. She was fed very basic food. She had her Bible, Prayer Book and copy of *The Imitation of Christ* as companions. She received hardly any visits and very few letters.

Prior to her imprisonment Edith Cavell had a daily agenda which included:

- managing her own staff and looking after patients at the *clinique*;
- managing the construction and other preparations for the new nurse training school nearby (going ahead despite difficult wartime conditions);
- hiding and nursing allied soldiers still being brought to her, and linking them up with guides;
- enduring unannounced searches at any time;
- looking after Grace Jemmett and Pauline Randall (see above, page 7)—and her dog, Jack.

Sleep, time alone and time with God would all have been scarce. She was exhausted.[30] And then, suddenly, she was in solitary confinement, for an indeterminate period and with no clarity about what might be the outcome.

Personal Reflection

Studies of long-term imprisonment, especially in terms of solitary confinement, report the frequency of prisoners quickly 'cracking up and becoming depressed and paranoid.'[31] What was happening to all her responsibilities in Brussels? How were her colleagues, also in prison, coping?[32] What of the marooned soldiers with no network now to help them?[33] How about her mother back home? She was powerless, cut off from colleagues facing trial and from her nurses still working outside the prison. How should she handle this sudden and unaccustomed time of quiet? How best should she make the most of each day? How in particular was she to control her thoughts about her own future?

She appears to have maintained her peace of mind. She reread Thomas à Kempis and no doubt reflected deeply on its themes of self-control, the need for all disciples of Christ to deepen their devotion to God, and the message that God is faithful, even in the face of death (Ps 23.4).

Uncertainty and powerlessness place enormous burdens on people confronting them (through illness, job loss or bereavement).

- How do I react to them myself? What can I learn from Edith Cavell?

We are increasingly unfamiliar with quiet today. We live in perpetual noisy connectedness to phones, music, media. There is no respite.

- What does this connectedness do to my time alone? What of time with God? Do I actively seek quietness…?

Linked Material

Cast your cares on the Lord and he will sustain you; he will never let the righteous be shaken. (Psalm 55.22, NIV)

The good man does not escape all troubles—he has them too. But the Lord helps him in each and every one. (Psalm 34.19, Living Bible)

Do not worry about your life, what you will eat or drink; or about your body, what you will wear. Is not life more than food, and the body more than clothes? Look at the birds of the air; they do not sow or reap or store away in barns, and yet your heavenly Father feeds them. Are you not much more valuable than them? (Matt 6.25–26)

Jesus frequently sought solitude (Matt 14.23 and 26.36), and encouraged his disciples to 'come to a quiet place and get some rest' (Mark 6.31).

8 'I May Have Been Strict, But I Loved You More Than You Know'[34]

[Beloved disciples…] are certainly sent not out to temporal joys, but to great conflicts; not to honours, but to contempts; not to idleness, but to labours; not to rest but to bring forth much fruit with patience.[35]

Edith Cavell wrote a farewell letter to her nurses from her cell.[36] She wanted to clear past wrongs and to encourage them, as she had done in through the years. She urges them, 'When better days come our work will again grow and resume all its power for doing good. I told you in our evening conversations that devotion would bring you true happiness and that the thought that before God you have done your duty well and with a good heart will sustain you in the hard moments of life and in the face of death.' The letter ends: 'I may have been strict, but I have loved you more than you can know.'

This is a powerful statement from a woman who exercised leadership and discipline for many years—often a lonely role. She may have *shown* she loved the nurses but may have found it hard to *state* this in public. It was the foundation of her life's work. Her love springs from her faith in God—the one who loved her from her earliest years—and that in turn shaped her service to her nurses, her patients and the Belgian people. 'Those who knew [Edith Cavell] never ceased to speak of her kindness, her consideration and her amazing patience…utterly, unbelievably unselfish, with an almost fanatical sense of duty. She expected the same from all those who worked with her.' (This may account for some feeling that she was 'cold, distant and aloof in her manner.')[37]

Personal Reflection

Nurses and soldiers operate within a framework of discipline, obedience to orders, team collaboration and loyalty. Respect and care undergird the relationships involved. It is only rarely that this extends to *love* for superiors or for those one leads. Holding together discipline, command and love is demanding.

- Do I love those I work with? Should I? How can I best express this?

Linked Material

Jesus gave them 'a new commandment, that you love one another…this is how people will know that you are my disciples' (John 13.34).

'I Have Seen Death So Often That It Is Not Strange or Fearful to Me'[38]

9

> What could the world offer you without Jesus? To be with Jesus is to know the sweetness of heaven. If Jesus is with you no enemy can harm you.[39]

Death was a constant companion to Edith Cavell through her nursing career. She supported many in their last hours, including men returned from the Boer Wars. Death hung in the air in 1914–1915 as the war raged.

Death as a *process* was familiar enough, as were the *causes* of death: disease, trauma and accident. What was unfamiliar to her personally was *execution*. Her own sentence brought her own imminent death into sharp focus. Perhaps she was expecting such an end to her life; the posters had warned of the consequences of sheltering allied soldiers. Nonetheless, the calm of her comment, 'I have seen death so often,' to the Rev'd Stirling Gahan in her meeting with him on her last night is remarkable.

Death and eternity will have been framed very starkly for both of them as they shared Jesus' Last Supper together in her cell. Gahan absolved her sins on God's behalf, praying, 'Almighty God…confirm and strengthen you in all goodness, and bring you to everlasting life.' The Creed concludes confidently, 'I look for the resurrection of the dead.' The Comfortable Words include the assurance that 'God so loved the world, that he gave his Son…to the end that all who believe in him [should] have everlasting life.' They shared bread and wine with the words, 'The Body of our Lord Jesus Christ…The Blood of our Lord Jesus Christ…shed for thee…preserve thy body and soul unto everlasting life.'[40]

They quietly repeated verses of the hymn *Abide with Me*, which, in the light of the prospect of the next morning, concludes poignantly:

> Hold Thou Thy cross before my closing eyes;/Shine through the gloom and point me to the skies. Heaven's morning breaks, and earth's vain shadows flee;/In life, in death, O Lord, abide with me.

Gahan's published account of their last moments together has *Edith* saying to him as he left her, 'We shall meet again' (clearly implying 'in heaven,' as she knew already he was not to be at her execution). Gahan's private manuscript version of their exchange differs: there he records that *he* said, as he shook her hand, 'We shall meet again,' and that she pressed his hand firmly, saying 'Yes, we shall.'[41] Whichever account is accurate is of little consequence—their mutual assurance of the reality of a new life beyond the firing squad is echoed in thousands of martyrdoms and deaths of faithful Christians down the centuries.

Personal Reflection

Professional distance may protect us from the impact of death. That impact may be lessened if we encounter it frequently at close quarters. But when it is our own death we are confronting, our thoughts bring our hopes and beliefs into sharp relief, especially what we believe about what may happen to us as the door of this earthly life closes on us.

- Is death, for me, the end? Or does it mark a new beginning?

Linked Material

Facing death and judgment, Job asserts, 'I know that my redeemer lives, and that in the end he will stand on the earth. And after my skin has been destroyed, yet in my flesh I will see God; I myself will see him with my own eyes—I, and not another. How my heart yearns within me!' (Job 19.25–27).

At Lazarus' grave, Jesus proclaims, 'I am the resurrection and the life. The one who believes in me will live, even though they die; and whoever lives by believing in me will never die' (John 11.25–26).

St Paul is absolutely confident: 'Christ Jesus who died—more than that, who was raised to life—is at the right hand of God and is also interceding for us… For I am convinced that neither death nor life, neither angels nor demons, neither the present nor the future, nor any powers, neither height nor depth, nor anything else in all creation, will be able to separate us from the love of God that is in Christ Jesus our Lord' (Rom 8.34, 38–39).

'Patriotism is Not Enough'[42]   10

> The splendour which is given to us and received by humanity is short-lived and sorrow is always its companion.[43]

After nearly three months of imprisonment, on Thursday 7 October all thirty-five prisoners involved in the underground network were brought before a German military tribunal. They were accused of 'conveying soldiers to the enemy,' which pitted one patriotism against another.

There was a lack of representation, limited translation and little room for pleas in mitigation. By the end of the second day the court adjourned to rule on the prosecutor's demand for the death sentence for nine of the group and long prison terms for many of the others. Other fellow prisoners broke down. Edith Cavell was impassive; she felt it useless to appeal. She said later, 'I am English and they want my life.'[44]

The evening of the day on which she learnt of her sentence the English chaplain visited her in her cell, late at night and unanticipated. With no preparation as a formal statement of her final thoughts, he records Edith ending by saying, 'Standing as I do in the light of God and eternity, I have realized that patriotism is not enough: I must have no hatred or bitterness towards anyone.'[45]

Personal Reflection

What does the phrase 'patriotism is not enough' really mean to her? We can only conjecture. The context is clear; she will have been well aware of three opposed allegiances:

German patriotism: Edith Cavell had encountered wounded German soldiers and their bewildered but tenacious adherence to their campaign. Many in the young German state felt that the rest of Europe and Russia were intent on marginalizing them and some believed that they had a mission to rescue Europe from growing decadence. They were determined to be masters in Belgium and to extinguish the fires of Belgian nationalism.

British patriotism: She had seen the gung-ho attitudes of some of the British soldiers she sheltered, as they came over the Channel to fight their country's cause. There was strong antagonism towards the 'Bloody Bosches,' the 'Damned Huns,' etc. There was a darker side to the patriotism in British imperialism, and defending British interests against German expansionism was one of the main points of international tension in the early 1900s.

Belgian patriotism: She knew how much damage had been caused to Belgium in the prosecution of the war, and of the bravery of the vastly outnumbered Belgian army. She knew of the anger at the rape of Namur and Louvain and of the mass killings of civilians there. She knew Belgians had died for daring to protest or act as spies out of patriotism.

After long reflection she concluded that *any* patriotism was '*not enough.*' Patriotism may seem laudable from one angle—but beneath its wing lurks ugly judgmentalism, xenophobia and even hatred. In all probability she would have accepted patriotism within limits as valid, even necessary, but not sufficient.

What is sufficient then? Maybe her answer lies in the Lord's Prayer: '*Our Father in heaven…*Your *kingdom come,* Your *will be done…*Yours *is the kingdom, the power and the glory*' (Matt 6.9–13). Any nationalistic patriotism, focused on one nation's interests, was, in a Christian understanding, under the judgment of an overarching kingdom, that of God and his justice and mercy. The Christian vision of God's peace and the flourishing of *all* men and women was countercultural in terms of contemporary nationalism and patriotism. Had the warring nations acknowledged their being subject to the rule of God in his world, they should not have been at each other's throats…

On 9 October 1915, in her copy of *The Imitation of Christ*, Edith Cavell marked the prayer, 'Scatter the nations that desire war. There is no other hope or refuge for me, save in thee, O Lord my God.'[46]

We may not be involved directly in international reconciliation and peace building. However, our responses to those from other cultures and even other sections of our own communities are often born out of fear and prejudice.

> • What does Edith Cavell teach me about my response to other nations and peoples? How can I assist building positive community relations?

Linked Material

In confronting the Jewish teachers of the Law over a case of threatened stoning for adultery, Jesus said, 'Let any one of you who is without sin be the first to throw a stone at her' (John 8.3–9).

Thomas à Kempis states, 'All things are transitory, including myself.' He prays, 'Above all, give me wisdom to search for you and to discern you, to know you and to love you, and to see all things as they really are and as you in your wisdom have arranged them.'[47]

'I Must Have No Hatred or Bitterness Towards Anyone'[48] 11

> We are only hindered and distracted [by the perverse ways of others] if we allow them to dominate us.[49]

Edith Cavell told Gahan in her cell that she must 'have no hatred or bitterness towards anyone.' Even towards the Germans who would execute her the next morning? Was she unhinged by her weeks in solitary confinement? Did the oppressors not deserve everything they got in the way of anger and resentment? Why was she not bitter that no one had intervened to save her—even God?

Gahan's private manuscript version of their interview reads, 'It is not enough to love one's own people: one must love all men and hate none.'[50] This even more positive rendering of the published version's 'no hatred or bitterness' echoes Jesus' command to his followers:

> You have heard that it was said, 'Love your neighbour and hate your enemy.' But I tell you, love your enemies and pray for those who persecute you, that you may be children of your Father in heaven. He causes his sun to rise on the evil and the good, and sends rain on the righteous and the unrighteous. (Matt 5.43–45)

Personal Reflection

Edith Cavell reiterates here a core value of the kingdom of God—forgiving others as we have been forgiven by God. She knew that Jesus had taught:

> If you forgive other people when they sin against you, your heavenly Father will also forgive you. But if you do not forgive others their sins, your Father will not forgive your sins. (Matt 6.14–15)

This seems a very hard saying when one thinks, for example, of some prisoners of war or holocaust survivors, or of some political prisoners and their children...

- Whom do I need to forgive? Whom have I not forgiven? With whom do I need to seek reconciliation?

Might Edith Cavell justifiably have felt bitterness towards God? She had, after all, been trying to be obedient to what she believed God required of her. She knew the risks; had God let her down? The answer probably lies in her understanding of the experience of her Lord in the Garden of Gethsemane awaiting his arrest.

Jesus went out as usual to the Mount of Olives, and his disciples followed him. He knelt down and prayed, 'Father, if you are willing, take this cup from me; yet not my will, but yours be done.' (Luke 22. 39–42)

• How do I deal with bitterness? How can I move from saying, 'My will be done' to 'Your will be done'?

Linked Material

St Paul says, 'Do not repay anyone evil for evil. Be careful to do what is right in the eyes of everyone. If it is possible, as far as it depends on you, live at peace with everyone. "If your enemy is hungry, feed him; if he is thirsty, give him something to drink. In doing this, you will heap burning coals on his head." Do not be overcome by evil, but overcome evil with good.' (Rom 12.17–18, 20–21).

Thomas à Kempis urges, 'Love everyone for Jesus' sake, but love Jesus for his own sake...He alone is the best and most faithful of friends. In him and for his sake, love both friend and enemy, and pray to him for all of them, in order that everyone may know and love him.'[51]

Resentment is like drinking poison and then hoping that it will kill our enemies.[52]

See also Archbishop Tutu's material on forgiveness.[53]

'I Die for God and for My Country'[54]

12

Grant me patience, O Lord, even in this emergency. Help me, and then I will not fear, however grievously I be afflicted. Lord, thy will be done.[55]

These were Edith Cavell's last words to the German chaplain (see chapter one). She died for God. This is entirely consistent with her lifelong Christian faith. God had called her to follow him, and to lay down her life for her friends as he had done. This was the culmination of her discipleship. As we have seen (chapter nine), she was not afraid of the journey through death to her God. She died for her country. Is this incongruous in the light of her statement on patriotism (chapter ten)? Or for her was the Allied cause most closely aligned with the goals of peace and justice of God's kingdom?

Personal Reflection

Three quarters of a million British male combatants died in WWI, along with 1,400 women, mainly UK nurses. Many in the armed forces are still dying for their country on behalf of others. Many Christians die for their faith.

- What cause—religious, spiritual, political—am I prepared to die for?

Edith Cavell's last letter to her nurses reads: '…the thought that before God you have done your duty well and with a good heart will sustain you in the hard moments of life and in the face of death…'

- In what ways can I echo Edith Cavell's clear sense that she was being obedient to the last?

Linked Material

Jesus said, 'My command is this: Love each other as I have loved you. Greater love has no one than this: to lay down one's life for one's friends.' (John 15.12–13). St Paul writes, 'Christ's love compels us, because we are convinced that one died for all…that those who live should no longer live for themselves but for him who died for them and was raised again' (2 Cor 5.14–15).

On the morning of 12 October, did Edith Cavell recall the reassurance of St Paul, 'The Lord is near. Do not be anxious about anything, but in every situation, by prayer and petition, with thanksgiving, present your requests to God. And the peace of God, which transcends all understanding, will guard your hearts and your minds in Christ Jesus' (Phil 4.5–7).

13 Conclusion: 'A Nurse Who Tried to Do Her Duty'[56]

> A person's achievements are often discussed, but rarely the qualities on which such a life is based.[57]

These words come from Edith Cavell's last meeting with Stirling Gahan. He had said, 'I shall always think of you as a heroine and martyr.' She sought to reframe his understanding of her—she was simply 'a nurse who tried to do her duty.'

Across the world many ignored her own self-evaluation and viewed her as a heroine, martyr, saint or icon. She was portrayed in propaganda as a young, vulnerable, attractive nurse—and there were calls for revenge for her martyrdom.[58]

Personal Reflection

How are we to see her and her journey to her death? Was she ultimately misguided and naïve? Was she seeking glory for herself, heedlessly jeopardizing her colleagues? This booklet has sought to get below the surface of the story and the woman to grasp how her beliefs informed her decisions.

She lived life on the understanding that she had a duty to God who had loved her so that she might love others. Her duty was to do God's work wherever she was placed by him. In war-weary Belgium, this meant saving lives as best she could, whatever the cost to herself. Her duty was to defy an oppressive regime and model a different and better kingdom.

A century later, many will see her execution as the end for Edith Cavell. She herself clearly saw it as a transition to a new beginning. She was committed to following a saviour who had died for her and countless other Christian disciples. His 'service was perfect freedom' and his reward was new life with him.

> • What lessons can I take from her life? Am I willing to follow her in imitating Christ?

Aftermath

There was public shock and outrage at the news of Edith Cavell's death. The first national memorial service was held on 29 October 1915, in St Paul's Cathedral. The Queen and Prime Minister attended. Queen Alexandra unveiled a statue of Edith Cavell in Norwich in October 1918.[59] After the end of hostilities Edith Cavell and countless others who died in WWI were commemorated. In May 1919, following a national memorial service at Westminster Abbey, her body was taken by train to Norwich and buried outside the cathedral. (The authorities had proposed that she should be buried in Westminster Abbey, an exceedingly rare offer. Her family felt it more appropriate that she be buried in Norwich).

For most people today only a dim memory of her lingers on. She is honoured by (mainly older) members of the nursing profession, and in Norfolk and Brussels. In 2015 we will see centenary commemorations of her worldwide.[60] Her life has a continuing practical impact through the Cavell Nurses' Trust, which was formed from public subscriptions to newspaper appeals after her death.[61] It works in the UK to support nurses and health care workers who fall on hard times, and to inspire the rising generation of nursing and midwifery students who show outstanding quality with scholarship awards.

Final Thoughts

'It is better to "fail" in a cause that will finally succeed than to "succeed" in a cause that will ultimately fail.' The Rev'd Bill Arlow, a Northern Ireland peace campaigner.

'He is no fool who gives what he cannot keep to gain that which he cannot lose.' Jim Elliott, missionary to the Auca tribe, diary entry, 28 October 1949. [62]

'To be "a witness" consists not in propaganda, nor even in stirring people up, but in being a living mystery. It means to live in such a way that one's life would not make sense if God did not exist.' Cardinal Suchard.[63]

Edith Cavell said in early August 1914, 'As nurses you must take no part in the quarrel. Our work is for humanity. The profession of nursing knows no frontiers.'[64]

'[Edith Cavell] was utterly, unbelievably unselfish' and had 'an almost fanatical sense of duty.'[65]

'I fear no foe with Thee at hand to bless…Where is death's sting?…I triumph still if Thou abide with me.' The final words of the hymn *Abide with Me,* shared with her chaplain on her last evening.

Notes

1   The most recent are Diana Souhami, *Edith Cavell* (London: Quercus, 2010); a shorter version is available as a Pitkin Guide (September 2014); and Terri Arthur, *Fatal Destiny: Edith Cavell WWI Nurse* (Milwaukee, WI: HenschelHAUS Publishing, 2014), a novel close to the historical detail. Earlier comprehensive UK biographies are: Rowland Ryder, *Edith Cavell* (London: Hamish Hamilton, 1975) and A E Clark-Kennedy, *Edith Cavell, Pioneer and Patriot* (London, Faber and Faber, 1965). All references to the Souhami biography (originally published in hardback in 2010) are to the paperback edition of 2011.

2   Thomas à Kempis was a German monk who in the 1420s wrote a four-part book, *Of the Imitation of Christ,* in Latin. An English version was given to Edith Cavell in 1890 when a governess, aged 24. Edith used this during her time at the London Hospital. A 1920 facsimile edition with her annotations of 1915 can be found at https://archive.org/details/ofimitationocave00londuoft. It is a very widely read devotional work; John Wesley urged all households to read it alongside the Bible.

3   Souhami, *op cit*, p 38.

4   This and similar introductory headers are taken from Thomas à Kempis's *The Imitation of Christ,* Robert Jeffery (trans) (London: Penguin, 2013), except where the original text as read by Edith Cavell in St Gilles prison from August–early October 1915 is used (*Of the Imitation of Christ: The 'Edith Cavell' edition* (tr unknown) (Oxford University Press, 1920). This is taken from the 1920 edition p 83 (Part III, ch 5). It is marked with double lines in her copy.

5   Ryder, *op cit*, p 14; Souhami, *op cit*, p 38.

6   By 1894 Lilian was training at St Thomas' Hospital in London, and Florence had also embarked on nursing.

7   Ryder, *op cit*, p 22.

8   Sister Wilkins, as cited in Souhami, *op cit*, p 131.

9   Souhami, *op cit*, p 78.

10 Souhami, *op cit*, p 63.

11 Ryder, *op cit*, p 40.

12 Ryder, *op cit*, p 80.

13 *The Imitation of Christ* (1920 ed), p 44 (Part I, ch 25). Marked in Edith Cavell's annotated copy.

14 Ryder, *op cit*, p 26.

15 In December 1910 Edith Cavell had invited her mother over to Brussels to see if she would prefer to live with her, rather than in her terraced home in College Road, Norwich. Mrs Cavell had opted to stay in Norwich (Souhami, *Edith Cavell*, p 135).

16 Souhami, *op cit*, p 163.

17 *The Imitation of Christ* (1920 ed), p 124 (Part III, ch 28). Marked in Edith Cavell's annotated copy.

18 Souhami, *op cit*, p 163.

19 Souhami, *op cit*, p 163.

20 Souhami, *op cit*, pp 180-184.

21 *The Imitation of Christ* (2013 ed) p 23 (Part I, ch 14).

22 Boger was captured in Brussels and interned in prisoner of war camps for most of the remainder of the war. Meachin got home safely, returning to active service in France.

23 *The Imitation of Christ* (1920 ed) p 58 (Part II, ch 6). Marked in Edith Cavell's own copy.

24 Souhami, *op cit*, pp 252 and 262.

25 *The Imitation of Christ* (1920 ed) p 58 (Part II, ch 1). Marked in Edith Cavell's own copy.

26 From the detailed list in Ryder, *Edith Cavell*, Appendix E, there are names for 25 men. Edith Cavell admitted to helping over 200 men in all up to July 1915. Thus it is likely that she had helped over 100 by May 1915.

27 Souhami, *op cit*, p 372. She added, 'It has been like a solemn fast from earthly distractions.'

28 *The Imitation of Christ* (2013 ed) p 67 (Part II, ch 9).

29 A manuscript report (see note 41) of the same evening by Stirling Gahan reads, 'I am thankful to have these ten weeks of quiet to get ready. Life was so full that I had no rest and no quiet—now I have had it.'

30 Her portrait of summer 1915 demonstrates it in her face. See www.edithcavell. org.uk

31 L Taylor and S Cohen, *Psychological Survival: the Experience of Long Term Imprisonment* (Harmondsworth: Penguin, 1972). See also E Debruyne and L van Ypersele, *Je Serai Fusillé Demain* (Brussels: Racine, 2011).

32 Two Belgians incarcerated in St Gilles were shot on 23 September. News of this will have carried round the corridors of St Gilles and added to the strain on all the group awaiting trial with Edith Cavell.

33 Some 4,000 soldiers, mainly Belgian and French, handed themselves in to the Germans following Edith Cavell's execution (Souhami, *op cit*, p 385).

34 Souhami, *op cit*, p 367. The letter was dated 10 October—Souhami suggests she edited it on 11 October, and that it was delivered after her death.

35 *The Imitation of Christ* (1920 ed) p 126 (Part III, ch 30). The whole chapter is marked in Edith Cavell's own copy, 'St Gilles, October 1915.'

36 She was unaware of the efforts of diplomats from the US and Spanish legations to get clarity from the authorities as to what had happened after the trial and to dissuade the German command from their resolve to execute her.

37 Noel Boston, *The Dutiful Edith Cavell* (Norwich: Norwich Cathedral, 1976) pp 8-9.

38 Souhami, *op cit*, p 372.

39 *The Imitation of Christ* (2013 ed) p 65 (Part II, ch 8). The whole chapter is highlighted by Edith Cavell in her own copy of *The Imitation of Christ* (1920 ed).

40 Quotations from the service of Holy Communion in the *Book of Common Prayer*.

41 In the possession of a member of the Cavell family, and kindly copied for the author.

42 Souhami, *op cit*, p 372.

43 *The Imitation of Christ* (2013 ed) p 61 (Part II, ch 6).

44 Souhami, *op cit*, p 353. See also note 36 above.

45 A manuscript report of the same evening by Stirling Gahan has a slightly different version of this statement; see chapter ten and note 41.

46 *The Imitation of Christ* (1920 ed) p 135 (Part III, ch 24).

47 *The Imitation of Christ* (2013 ed) p 169 (Part III, ch 27).

48 Souhami, *op cit*, p 372.

49 *The Imitation of Christ* (2013 ed) p 55 (Part II, ch 1).

50 See note 41.

51 *The Imitation of Christ* (2013 ed) p 65 (Part II, ch 8): 'On having Jesus as an intimate friend.' The whole chapter was marked in Edith Cavell's 1920 edition.

52 This quote has been attributed to Nelson Mandela but see http://www.barrypopik.com/index.php/new_york_city/entry/resentment_is_like_drinking_poison

53 Desmond and Mpho Tutu, *The Book of Forgiving* (New York: Harper Collins, 2014) and The Forgiveness Challenge (www.forgivenesschallenge.com).

54 Souhami, *op cit*, p 377.

55 *The Imitation of Christ* (1920 ed) p 125. The chapter, 'How we ought to call upon God, and to bless him, when tribulation is upon us' is marked 'St Gilles October 1915,' and this section is highlighted.

56 Souhami, *op cit*, p 373.

57 *The Imitation of Christ* (2013 ed) p 175 (Part III, ch 31).

58 The British government made much of her death in encouraging volunteers to join the army. For the six weeks following her death numbers of recruits signing up doubled to nearly 12,000 a week (Ryder, Appendix D).

59 With another by St Martin-in-the-Fields in London in 1923. Both were paid for by public subscription.

60 See www.edithcavell.org.uk

61 Cavell Nurses Trust website: www.cavellnursestrust.org

62 Journal entry, perhaps derived from Philip Henry (father of Matthew Henry, the Bible commentator): 'He is no fool who parts with that which he cannot keep, when he is sure to be recompensed with that which he cannot lose.'

63 Cited in Sam Wells, *Learning to Dream Again* (London: SPCK, 2012) p 48.

64 Souhami, *op cit*, p 163.

65 Boston, *op cit*, p 9.